BIKE AND SU

MICK WOOLLETT

From the ubiqu
road-going supe
contemporary m
traces the histor
present day, then individually discusses today's
lightweights, the superbikes, road-racing machines
(including endurance and drag racing), off-road
competition machines (including motocross,
speedway, grass-track, trials and ice racing), and
finally the choppers, stunt bikes and show bikes.
Twenty-four full colour illustrations depict the
latest and most exciting machines on the scene
today.

Mick Woollett is editor of *Motor Cycle*, Britain's
leading motorbike weekly, and a respected and
well-known technical journalist.

64 pages
23 colour photographs
23 black and white photographs

BIKE AND SUPERBIKE

Mick Woollett

The world's fastest
production sports model is the
1000cc Laverda from Italy

B T Batsford Ltd. London

ISBN 0 7134 0540 6

Set in 11/13pt 'Monotype' Plantin
Printed in Hong Kong by Colorcraft Ltd.
for the publishers B T Batsford Limited
4 Fitzhardinge Street, London W1H 0AH

Contents

Acknowledgment

Many of the photographs are from the author's own collection; for permission to use other photographs in this book thanks are due to the following individuals and organisations: *Motor Cycle*, Cecil Bailey, Don Morley, Keith Lee, Geoff Statham, Alan Maguire, John Nutting, Jan Heese and Brian Nicholls.

The early bikes

Every schoolboy knows that Stephenson invented the railway locomotive, and Gottlieb Daimler built the first motor cycle, and . . . but hey, whoa! It was not that simple, you know.

There were plenty of steam locomotives puffing around before George Stephenson came on the scene. And plenty of people had tried their hands at powered two- and three-wheelers before Daimler came along. For instance, somewhere near the start of it all was the steam-driven Micheaux-Perreaux boneshaker of 1869; and then there was an American named Lucius D. Copeland, who applied steam power to a penny-farthing (or to be more accurate a farthing-penny, because the smaller wheel was at the front), at the thought of which the mind boggles.

No, where Gottlieb Daimler comes into the picture is that he was the first to produce a (relatively) lightweight internal combustion engine, running at the (relatively) high speed of 800 rpm on petrol-gas fuel. This he patented in 1884 and, a year later, a version of Daimler's engine was installed in an extremely crude wooden frame – supported by two outrigger wheels – and made to drive the wooden rear wheel through gearing.

It was but a means to an end, and after Daimler proved that the idea worked he turned his attention to cars, leaving the development of the true motor cycle to others.

Almost certainly the first motor cycle to be produced in any quantity (and here we are talking of tens, rather than thousands) was the Hildebrand and Wolfmuller of 1894 which, in some ways, was quite an advanced design. The engine was a horizontal parallel twin, with water-cooled cylinders, and the cooling water was carried in a curved tank which served, also, as the rear mudguard. However, the connecting rods drove directly on to cranks on the rear wheel spindle and, because there was no fly-wheel, flat rubber bands were used to help return the connecting rods on the idle stroke.

The bicycle industry was already well-established when the first motor cycles began to putter onto the roads, and it was natural that the big companies – Raleigh, Ariel, Royal Enfield and others – should experiment with applying power to their pedal machines.

The trouble was that nobody was *quite* sure where the engine should go. Royal Enfield, for example, mounted it in front of the steering head, but then used it to drive the rear wheel by a long, crossed round-leather belt. Raleigh carried the engine in the same place, but used it to drive the front wheel. Ormonde mounted it just ahead of the rear wheel, where the gear box of a modern machine is located. One maker (Shaw) carried it on an outrigger frame *behind* the rear wheel, with a belt driving forward.

It was a pair of Russian emigré brothers in Paris, the Werners, who first pointed the way. They, too, had begun by mounting the engine ahead of the steering column, but in 1902 came a move to a more logical position. The new Werner 2 hp model of that year carried the crankcase in what would be the bottom bracket position of a pedal cycle, so giving a vastly improved weight distribution and a corresponding freedom from the dreaded side-slip.

Where the Werners led, others soon followed, and before long the number of motor cycle 'factories' had multiplied manifold. This expan-

The 1929 490cc overhead-camshaft Norton

Paul Foulkes Halbard's 998cc Indian, which was ridden by A H Alexander in the 1912 Tourist Trophy race

sion was helped along by the increasing number of proprietary engine makers, mainly of Continental origin, including Aster, Minerva, De Dion, and Kelecom. Other companies, including BSA and Chater-Lea were already in business manufacturing and supplying frame-leg sets, and so it was a simple matter for a local ironmonger or blacksmith to construct a few frames, clamp engines to them, apply a fancy transfer, and call himself a motor cycle maker.

So let us look at a typical motor cycle of the early 1900s. It would be direct belt drive from engine to rear wheel (no clutch, and no gear box). The engine would be a four-stroke, but only the exhaust valve would be operated by a cam and the inlet valve would be 'automatic', which implied that it was fitted with a very light valve spring, and would open to allow fresh gas into the cylinder, by suction as the piston descended.

The carburation, too, would be vague, for although the spray carburettor was just beginning to come in, the machine would be more likely to have a so-called surface carburettor – nothing more than a shallow tray of fuel, agitated by the motion of the bike, the vapour from which would be collected by a draught passing across the surface. Ignition? This could be platinum-bulb made incandescent by application of an external flame; or, more sophisticated, coil ignition by way of a trembler coil which emitted a shower of sparks, some of which were bound to occur at roughly the right place in the cycle!

It was the coming of the Tourist Trophy Races (the Isle of Man TT) which did more than anything else to advance the cause of the motor cycle. The significance of the Tourist Trophy name was that the races were intended to prove and develop *touring* machines, rather than the

The first BMW offered for sale was a sensation at
the Paris show in 1923

monstrous devices – huge engines in flimsy
frames – that had been concocted for the short,
banked-track races of the Continent.

Right from the start of the series in 1907, the
Triumph company decided to dispense with the
auxiliary pedalling gear that other makers had
considered essential. Spray-type carburettors
became universal, spring forks replaced the
original strutted, rigid types, and more robust
tyres were developed to cope with the rough,
untarred roads.

As engines became more powerful, so gearing
became necessary, to permit them to run at their
most efficient shaft speed whatever the going,
but at first there were a number of blind alleys to
be explored. Many makers (among them
Triumph) opted for what was really a beefed-up
version of the cyclist's rear-hub gear, but space
considerations meant that the parts had, of

necessity, to be flimsy. Further blind alleys were
those into which the Rudge and Zenith companies wandered, with their respective systems
(*Rudge Multi* and *Zenith Gradua*) of providing a
variety of ratios by opening or closing the sides
of the vee-belt pulleys on the engine shaft and
rear wheel.

A further stimulus to the development of the
motor cycle came with World War One, during
which many thousands of motor cycles – mainly
of Douglas, Triumph, Phelon and Moore, Clyno
and BSA origin – were used for despatch riding,
often in atrocious conditions. By this time the
science of metallurgy had improved tre-
mendously, and with the advent of better metals
the motor cycle became more efficient.

Yet there was still a very long way to go. The
average motor cycle of the early 1920s was a
single-cylinder side-valve, and two-strokes

(pioneered largely by Levis and Connaught) were thought of as slow, cheap, ride-to-work utility mounts, rather like the moped of today.

Just here and there, however, could be discerned the glimmerings of fresh thought. Sun-Vitesse, of Birmingham, appeared at Brooklands in 1920, and in the TT the following June, with a two-stroke engine which embodied a disc valve within the crankcase – similar in principle, though not in execution, with those of German and Japanese racing mounts of thirty to forty years later.

For that matter, the TT had been won in 1912 by a water-cooled, rotary-valve, two-stroke twin (the Scott, of course) but there the rotary valve was really a distributor barrel, interposed between carburettor and crankcase, and driven from the engine shaft, at first by chain and later by gears.

The early 1920s, too, brought the first stirring of a four-valve overhead-valve movement, when Triumph invoked the assistance of Harry Ricardo in evolving a high-efficiency engine. True, the 'Riccy' was to earn a reputation as an uncertain handler, but that was because the makers installed the engine in a frame originally designed for a much less potent power unit. British Anzani went one better than Triumph by producing a vee-twin 1000cc engine with four valves per cylinder. Rudge made a four-valver (the first of a very long line) and added gilt to the gingerbread by coupling it to the first production four-speed gear box. That was in 1925, by which time vee-belt drive had been displaced by chain on all except the very cheapest of utility runabouts.

So what about shaft drive? Well, Belgium's famous FN armament works had been building shaft-drive motor cycles (four-cylinder, at that!) since around 1905. America's very similar Pierce-Arrow happened along in 1911. And from Germany, in 1923, came perhaps the most familiar of all shaft-drive machines, the transverse flat-twin BMW.

Even in Britain there had been occasional attempts – rather half-hearted, it must be said – to produce a shaft-drive machine. The triers included GSD (Grant Shaft Drive) of Coventry, Berwick-Villiers of Banbury, and, a little later, Exeter's AJW company and Douglas, staunch adherents of the flat-twin engine, with their Endeavour.

Right through the 1920s, often termed the Golden Age of Motor Cycling, the motor cycle was taking definitive shape. Total-loss oiling of four-stroke models, at one time universal, gradually gave way before the advance of circulatory systems such as those pioneered by Royal Enfield (1913 on) and Bradshaw (1922 on). Beaded-edge tyres, which clung to the rims by virtue of a heavy beading of rubber and canvas, began to be replaced by stronger, wire-edged tyres from around 1906.

Initially, following the example of the pedal cycle, oil lamps had been employed for night-time riding (perilous though such a voyage might be, what with wandering farm animals, and unlit carts left standing in the roadway). But by 1908 gas lighting was in the ascendancy, fed by a small container, attached to the motor cycle, in which water was allowed to drip onto calcium carbide lumps, to produce acetylene gas. It was left to America's celebrated Indian marque to produce the first motor cycle equipped as standard with an efficient electric lighting system in 1914. Britain's legendary ABC flat-twin (among its attributes was an efficient swinging-arm rear suspension) was equipped with electric lighting from the outset in 1919.

Certainly by the end of the 1920s, the motor cycle had become, very recognisably, the ancestor of today's machine. The old-fashioned flat petrol tank had been replaced by a smoothly rounded saddle tank following the fashion set by Ariel and HRD. Cellulose paintwork, instead of oil-based enamel, was already available in 1928 on the little Baker-Villiers. And chromium-plating had made its appearance (on, of all things, a Rudge speedway model) for 1929; chrome, at this time, was tricky stuff and, to ensure a perfect finish, the Rudge people took

Often called the 'Rolls Royce' of motorcycles, the 1929 680cc Brough Superior Black Alpine

A typical sidecar outfit of the early 1920s; a Matchless V twin

A racing bike of the early '30s, the 1933 500cc Sunbeam

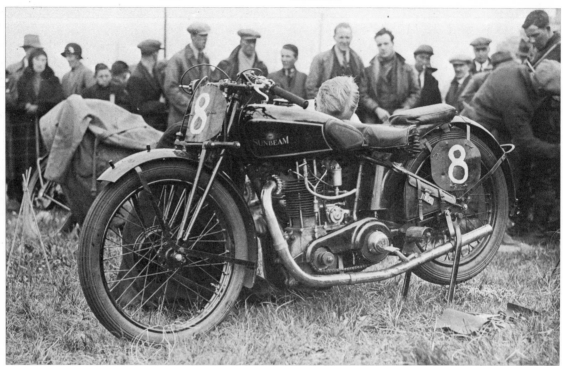

the precaution of sending all the bright bits to a Sheffield cutlery firm for plating.

Back in the days of World War One, despatch riders had taken to bending the hand-gear-change levers of their Triumphs to a horizontal position so that the gears could be changed with the foot, so leaving the hands free to concentrate on the job of steering through the Flanders mud (on the Sturmey-Archer gear boxes of the Triumphs, the gear lever was mounted directly on the end cover, instead of on the tank side, which made things easier). True, it was crude, with the middle of the three ratios a matter of hit-or-miss; but it was reasonably effective.

All the same, true foot-change was some way off, and when it *did* come, it was due to Velocette race-shop wizard Harold Willis, who, after studying the action of a shaping machine in the workshop, modified the principle so that it formed the first positive-stop mechanism. Velocettes so equipped made their debut in the 1927 Junior TT, and their superiority was such that everybody immediately set to work, evolving positive-stop systems of their own.

Telescopic front forks? BMW and, later, Norton, used those for racing in the 1930s. And by 1938 Velocette had a rear springing system very much like today's in appearance. It's like they say; it's all been done before. Maybe not as *well* done, but there – it is all a matter of progress.

Today's Lightweights

Time was when a lightweight motor cycle was a poor thing, an economy model aimed at providing cheap transport for the masses with no concession to style or performance.

What a different picture today! Now the choice of sophisticated lightweights, often fitted with many desirable gadgets as standard, is bewildering.

Basically they still provide inexpensive transport. They can cost less than one fifth the price of the cheapest four-wheeler and equally important they are cheap to put on the road, cheap to service and in a world increasingly energy conscious, they will cover incredible distances on a tankful of fuel.

Smallest and least expensive of the lightweights is the humble moped. Curiously, legislation has helped to boost the sales of these machines particularly in Great Britain.

A few years ago, when everyone over sixteen could legally ride a motor cycle the moped with its 50cc engine and pedals was looked down on by any youngster who fancied himself as a motor cyclist. He would not be seen dead on a vehicle associated, in those days, with district nurses and elderly workers.

Yamaha's trend-setter, the FS1E 50cc sports moped

Then the government stepped in, raised the age limit for riding a motor cycle to seventeen but decreed that sixteeners could still ride 50cc machines provided that they were 'capable of being self-propelled by pedals'.

The dealers forecast disaster. Instead the government created a boom. For overnight they erased the 'cissy' stigma of the moped. Suddenly all sixteeners were equal. It was a moped or nothing . . . and few boys (or girls) like to walk.

Never slow to exploit an opening the manufacturers, led by the Japanese big three of Honda, Yamaha and Suzuki, produced special models to cater for the new market. Initially the best-seller was the FS1E Yamaha. A two-stroke, it had a higher top speed (over 40 mph) than the four-stroke Honda – a vital sales point with a teenage market. Slower off the mark Suzuki had time to have a long cool look at the opposition and in 1976 they launched their AP50. It was an immediate success.

These machines are classified as sports mopeds. They feature four or five speed gear-boxes with conventional motor-cycle style foot-change, big brakes, proper suspension fore and aft and adequate lights.

The old bugbear of pedalling to start has been done away with by fitting a kick-start. For the engines, though small, now produce more than enough power for standing start, clutch get-aways.

In essence these are lightweight motor cycles fitted with pedals to comply with the law – and the pedals are seldom if ever used. In fact they swivel and lock into position opposite one another so that the rider can use them as conventional footrests and does not have to ride with one foot up and one down.

Many countries, and Great Britain will almost certainly follow suit, restrict mopeds to a certain maximum speed, often 40 kmh (28 mph). Manufacturers achieve this lower performance by fitting alternative cylinder barrels (in the case of two-strokes), cylinder heads (four-strokes) and carburettors.

In many countries these low performance two-strokes can be ridden without a licence or even insurance by anyone over fourteen.

Stepping up from the sports moped (the basic mopeds are more akin to bicycles and are outside the scope of this book) the motor-cycle field splits into two: the straightforward road-going models and the increasingly popular trail machines.

The latter are designed to be ridden both on the road and on unsurfaced tracks. They are ideal for exploring the countryside and first became popular in the United States where the motor cycle, due initially to clever marketing tactics by the big Japanese manufacturers, has caught on in a big way as a leisure and pleasure vehicle.

King of the lightweight commuter bikes is the 125cc Honda. This is powered by a beautifully engineered, single-cylinder four-stroke engine with chain driven single overhead cam-shaft.

Bore and stroke are 56×49.5 mm and the little engine revs to an incredible 9,000 rpm at which speed it whacks out 14 horse power – enough to propel it at close to 70 mph.

Specification is luxurious and includes rev-counter as well as a speedo, direction indicators, dual seat with pillion footrests, brake stop-light coupled to both front and rear brake systems, neutral indicator light and helmet lock. All for

Introduced at the 1976 Earl's Court Show, the
latest Honda lightweight, the CG125

a price little above that of a sports moped!

Yamaha, Suzuki and Kawasaki all sell single cylinder two-stroke equivalents – and Suzuki also market a very swift little 125cc twin. Named the GT125, this will top 70 mph under favourable conditions with the neat little parallel twin engine revving to 10,000 rpm. No wonder they fit a hydraulic front disc brake as standard!

The trail bike variants are all powered by suitably modified single cylinder engines mounted in special frames. These give more clearance for covering rough ground and have an upright riding position, designed to give the rider greater control at lower speeds where balance becomes an important factor. For, strange to say, one of the greatest assets that a trail bike can have is the ability to go as slowly as possible – the opposite of that demanded from a sports roadster.

At the same time the trail bike must be able to cruise at a reasonable pace on the open road so, as in all things, a compromise has to be reached.

A single cylinder engine is preferred because of its lighter weight and more flexible power characteristics. The Japanese big-four of Honda, Yamaha, Suzuki and Kawasaki (who between them produce around 4,000,000 motor cycles a year) dominate this market, their sheer volume of production making it extremely difficult for any other makers to match them on price or quality.

While motor cycles now come in all sorts of engine capacities, the next main class is the 250cc – the top division of the lightweight category.

Top selling sports roadsters in this class are the two-stroke twins offered by Suzuki and Yamaha. Both produce around 30 brake horse power, enough to get very close to the magic ton and perhaps even top it if the wind is in the right direction.

The high performance two-stroke engines give tremendous acceleration, helped by five and six speed gearboxes.

Kawasaki too have a powerful challenger in their KH250, the smallest in their range of high performance, three-cylinder two-strokes. This has searing acceleration though slightly less top speed than the twins – and an incredible thirst for petrol with fuel consumption dropping as low as 30 mpg if the rider really gets into the swing of things!

In recent years Honda have opted out of the sports market to concentrate on solid, reliable, economical four-strokes.

The hard-pressed European manufacturers still have a foothold in this class. In Italy Benelli and the Harley-Davidson subsidiary at Varese both market attractive two-fifties, the Benelli a twin, the Harley a single.

Owned by industrialist Alejandra de Tomaso, Benelli and Moto Guzzi also have plans for very sophisticated, four-cylinder four-stroke models. These will share the same neatly engineered overhead camshaft engines with slight styling changes to differentiate between them.

These new fours were first shown at the Milan exhibition in 1975 but a year later there are still no definite marketing plans.

At the economy end of the market the Eastern European manufacturers have a firm foothold. The East German MZ factory have a reputation for value-for-money, single-cylinder, two-strokes backed by successes in the International Six Days Trial and in road racing where their disc valve 250cc twin set the fashion in the

A favourite from East Germany, the 1976
MZ TS250

late fifties by proving conclusively that the new
generation of two-strokes could beat the four-
strokes: a lesson the Japanese were quick to
note.

The Czech Jawa factory too have built up a
following for their no-nonsense range of two-
strokes and now the Russians, under their
Cossack trademark, are trying hard to break into
the market.

But the lightweight market still belongs to the
Japanese makers. They fostered it and produced
eye-catching, beautifully engineered models that
not only perform extremely well but also keep
on performing and give very little trouble; a key
point in today's world when the price of labour
and spares has shot through the roof.

The top-selling 250 on the British market, the
GT250 Suzuki

The Superbikes

The superbike is a modern phenomenon. Costing more than a car, and able to exceed most legal speed limits in second or third gear, it flies in the face of logic and, in a way, of authority too. And this perhaps is its charm. It is for the person with an adventurous streak in his personality – for someone who every now and then wants to get away from it all.

The surprising thing is that there are far more of these people than the manufacturers ever dreamed existed! The European makers had been conditioned to think that the motor cycle was an economy vehicle bought by people who could not afford four-wheelers.

Certainly there have always been a handful of makers who built luxury machines, firms such as Brough Superior, Vincent, and BMW, but their top models sold only in small numbers and only to committed enthusiasts, people who had been motor cyclists for years and wanted the best in quiet, powerful bikes.

As with so many things, it was the Americans who started the superbike swing. Brought up on big, vee-twin Harley-Davidsons and Indians, they demanded big, lazy engines which would give trouble-free service on their long, straight roads.

So in the fifties the British makers, becoming more and more dependent on the then slowly expanding Stateside market, began to build their first quantity production superbikes – though that term was not coined until some years later.

By today's standards their specifications were modest, 600cc and 650cc twins. But they could top 100 mph and they were big, sports motor cycles designed for the man who wanted performance – and who was prepared to pay for it.

The market for such machines steadily grew, helped by the economic changes that have boosted the pay of the younger workers so that their purchasing power is now closer to that of their seniors.

This growth in interest in high-powered, high-performance machines took place at the time when the Japanese industry was expanding rapidly. Initially, the Japanese based their market on high-quality lightweights, but as sales zoomed they moved steadily up the capacity ladder.

In 1968 Honda announced what was arguably the first of the modern generation of superbikes – the CB750. With its four-cylinder, overhead-camshaft, race-bred engine it was an instant success and thousands have been sold the world over.

The specification included electric starting and a five-speed gearbox. The design was so sound that over the years few changes have been made, and apart from the addition of disc brakes and styling changes the 750cc Honda still sets a standard by which to judge all other super-bikes.

Inspired by the Japanese and the British, whose 750cc three-cylinder BSA and Triumph models were introduced in 1969, the Germans and Italians joined the superbike race. Like the British they reasoned that, whereas the Japanese had cornered the market for the lightweight classes, they could compete in the big-bike area where mass production was less of a factor, and where profit margins per machine were considerably higher.

Now, ironically, the Japanese, Italians and

Two 400cc roadsters from Kawasaki; on the left
the new four-stroke twin, and on the right the
three-cylinder two-stroke

Germans all have thriving factories making superbikes while the British, who can claim to have started the trend, are struggling for survival!

Before going on to discuss the current big-bike scene it is worthwhile trying to define a superbike. This is no easy task, but basically it must be of large engine capacity (say 650cc minimum), must have outstanding performance coupled to good handling and brakes and, equally important, it must look the part.

Of the Japanese factories all but Yamaha market at least two machines that fall within this definition. Kawasaki lead the field with three. Flagship of their range is the new 1000cc double-overhead-camshaft four-cylinder, an up-rated version of the world-famous Kawasaki Z900, winner of several 'Bike of the Year' awards in both the British and world motor-cycle press.

These big four-cylinder Kawasaki engines have earned a reputation for rugged reliability, and ruled the roost in the endurance racing field until the Honda factory entered their pukka factory team, equipped with experimental 940cc machines, in the class in 1976.

Top speed of the original Z900 was just over the 130 mph mark so the 1000cc version should be good for around 135 mph in standard form. The next model in the Kawasaki line-up is the KZ750 twin, designed as a luxury tourer rather than an out-and-out sports machine, but still capable of 110 mph.

To fill the gap between the large capacity

The 1976 Kawasaki Z650 was the first four-cylinder of this capacity

Honda's biggest model, the luxury tourer Gold
Wing GL1000

machines and the lightweights the third
Kawasaki superbike, introduced late in 1976, is
something no one else has ever marketed before,
a four-cylinder 650cc sports model. This is
powered by a completely redesigned engine.
With bore and stroke of 62 × 54 (giving an exact
capacity of 652cc) it achieves an impressive 64
brake horse power at 8,500 rpm, to give a top
speed of close to 120 mph. Kawasaki have made
a real effort to keep the 650 compact, low and
light. And they have succeeded reasonably well
with a weight of 465 lbs.

Honda, first of the Japanese factories to enter
the superbike field, offer two genuine models
with a back-up of smaller four-cylinder models

(400cc and 550cc) which fall just short of our
definition.

Biggest of the range, and superb value for
money, is the Gold Wing. Powered by a water-
cooled, car-style 1000cc engine, the Gold
Wing is unbeatable among the touring, as
opposed to sporting, superbikes. The engine is
completely different to any other motor-cycle
unit. Very similar in layout to that of the Alfa
Sud car it is a flat-four with two cylinders on
one side and two on the other (like a four-
cylinder BMW).

Bore and stroke are very oversquare at
72 × 51.4 mm (giving 999cc). Compression ratio
is 9.2, and despite its weight of 570 lbs the Gold

Wing has a sprightly performance with a top speed of 130 mph and wheel-spinning acceleration. One of its assets is shaft drive. Perfected on motor cycles by BMW, the shaft is not as mechanically efficient as a well adjusted roller-chain, but it needs no maintenance and never needs replacing.

Honda's smaller superbike is the more sporting air-cooled, four-cylinder CB750F. The latest in a line of 750cc Hondas descended from the original CB750 (which remains in production for some markets), the F model has a four-into-one exhaust system and rakishly styled tank and seat.

As with the Gold Wing, disc brakes are fitted front and rear. The classic in-line across the frame engine is unusual now in having a slightly longer stroke than bore (63 mm stroke to 61 mm bore) with an exact capacity of 736cc. Weight is a hefty 530 lbs, but despite this the Honda will cruise at around 100 mph and has a top speed of 115 mph.

Alone among the manufacturers, Suzuki market both two-stroke and four-stroke superbikes. The well established GT750 is powered by a water-cooled, three-cylinder two-stroke engine set across the frame.

With bore and stroke of 70×64 (738cc) the engine produces 70 bhp at a relatively leisurely 6,500 rpm. Gearbox is a five-speeder and this delightfully quiet and well mannered superbike has tremendous acceleration and a top speed of around 112 mph.

The four-stroke Suzuki, the first poppet valve engine to be introduced by Suzuki who previously concentrated on two-strokes and the rotary valve Wankel, is the GS750, first unveiled in August 1976. This is a conventional four-cylinder, in-line, across the frame layout of the type pioneered commercially by Honda and later taken up by Kawasaki.

Having decided to tackle Honda and Kawasaki on their own ground, Suzuki will have to do better than their established rivals if they are to do well. Suzuki have concentrated on keeping weight and size to the minimum, and on neat styling. The outcome is a pleasingly sleek machine. The double-overhead-camshaft engine, with bore and stroke of 65×56.4 mm, develops 68 horse power at 8,500 rpm, and Suzuki claim a top speed of 124 mph. They have already promised a 1000cc version for the near future.

There is a third Suzuki superbike, the Wankel-engined RE-5, but this has not been a success so far and may be phased out of the range.

The RE-5 was the first superbike with a rotary-type engine to be marketed and some feel that it was rushed into production so that it could go on sale ahead of any rival Wankel designs. The large and ungainly-looking engine has a single rotor – and, like all Wankels so far produced, the fuel consumption is heavy. It was Suzuki's bad luck that the RE-5 was launched just before the energy crisis hit the world and focused attention on miles per gallon!

Yamaha are the last of the Japanese factories to step into the superbike arena. They made the first tentative steps a few years ago when they introduced a 750cc twin; but this was a disaster and was soon withdrawn.

Now they are back with what looks to be a winner – a three-cylinder, overhead-camshaft four-stroke with five-speed gearbox and shaft drive. Named the XS750, the Yamaha challenger is compact, and clever styling helps to make it look far smaller than its four-cylinder rivals.

A British superbike, the three-cylinder 750cc
Triumph Trident

Of the European factories BMW of Germany produce the largest number of superbikes. They currently offer superbikes in two capacities: 1000cc, and 750cc. Both follow the classic BMW design pattern laid down in 1923 when the Munich factory (founded during the first world war to make aero engines for the German air-force) first entered the motor-cycle market – twin-cylinder, horizontally opposed, four-stroke engines with shaft drive.

Unveiled late in 1976 the 1000cc range, headed by the R100/RS which comes complete with streamlined fairing, is powered by the biggest motor-cycle engine BMW have ever made. With bore and stroke of 94×70.6 mm, it punches out 70 horse power at 7,250 to give this distinctive machine a top speed of over 120 mph. It is also the most expensive superbike in quantity production, costing (depending on where bought) around twice as much as the comparable 1000cc Honda Gold Wing!

Although their output is limited, the Italians have more manufacturers building superbikes than any other country – five, to be precise.

Most famous of these are MV Agusta, whose racing machines have won more grand prix races than any others. Their superbike is the 750S, powered by a road going version of the four-cylinder, double-overhead-camshaft racing engine that won them fame in the fifties and sixties. This robust unit (67×56 mm) attains around 85 horse power at 8,500 rpm and drives the rear wheel via a five-speed gearbox and shaft

At around £3000 the BMW R100/RS is the world's most expensive roadster

Yamaha's first four-stroke superbike, the
double-overhead-cam, three-cylinder 750cc

drive, a nice refinement on such an out-and-out
sporting machine.

The Italian makers claim a top speed of close
to 140 mph but tests in Britain suggest that the
maximum is nearer to 125 mph. Suffice it to
say that when it comes to appearance the scar-
let, blue and white MV Agusta is probably
the most impressive two-wheeler on the market.

Fastest of the superbikes is almost certainly
the 1000cc Laverda Jota (*see frontispiece*).
This double-overhead-camshaft, three-cylinder
Italian sports bike has been electronically timed
by the British weekly *Motor Cycle* at 140 mph –
double the legal limit on British motorways!
Underlining its superiority, it is also a favourite
for production machine racing because that
speed is allied to wonderful handling.

The vee-twin Ducati 900SS is another noted
for fine roadholding. The impressive engine
(86×74.4 mm) has desmodromic valve gear
(valves closed mechanically instead of by
springs) and the vee-twin layout leads to a small
frontal area and a low centre of gravity. With
clever designing, the Italians have managed to
keep the weight down to 425 lbs, considerably
lighter than any of the Japanese superbikes.

The Moto Guzzi 750-S3 is also powered by
a vee-twin but in this case the engine is mounted
across the frame. This layout lends itself to
shaft-drive. Power of the 82.5×70.2 unit is
70 bhp at a lazy 7,000 rpm – giving a top speed of
around 120 mph.

No lack of variety from the Italians! In fact
all five of their superbikes have a different engine

Reg Pridmore on a BMW production racer in action at Daytona

The sleek powerhouse of the Suzuki GT550

Impressive tourer from Italy, the V twin 850 T3
Moto Guzzi

layout – and the most way-out of them all is the 750cc Benelli. This is powered by a six-cylinder engine, unique in motor cycling.

The engine is an air-cooled, in-line six (56 × 50.6) with single-overhead-camshaft valve operation. Gearbox is a five-speeder and final drive is by chain. Weight has been kept down to a creditable 485 lbs, but the six-cylinder engine does make it a wide bike.

From the once mighty British industry comes a trickle of 850cc Norton Commandos and 750cc Triumph Tridents – with the planned possibility of a 900cc version of the Trident.

The Norton is powered by a vertical twin, pushrod engine (58 bhp at 6,000) and has a four-speed gearbox. A feature is that the engine and separate gearbox are rubber mounted.

With a more modern design, the engine of the Triumph is far more impressive, the three cylinders set in-line across the frame.

In the early seventies racing versions of this pushrod (67 × 70) unit gained worldwide fame on the race circuits and in 1971 finished 1-2-3 in the Daytona 200, America's most important race.

The five-speed gearbox is in unit and the 1976 model is neatly styled; among the superbikes it is one of the most economical, able to cover over 50 miles per gallon.

It was the demands of the American market

Probably the most handsome of the superbikes is
the four-cylinder 750S MV Agusta

Latest from the States is the sleekly styled
Harley-Davidson FXE 1200

that started the superbike swing and no list would be complete without Harley-Davidson, sole survivor of the once vigorous American motor-cycle industry.

Currently the Milwaukee factory build three models that fall into the superbike category. The smallest of these is the new XL 1000 Sportster. Like all the big Harleys it is powered by a massive overhead valve vee-twin engine. With bore and stroke of 81 × 96.8 (997cc) this produces 61 horse power at 6,200 rpm to give a top speed of 110 mph.

With similar sporting lines the FX 1200 is the big brother of the XL 1000. The larger (1,207cc) engine emits a claimed 66 horse power at a lowly 5,200.

Fitted with the same engine the FLH 1200 Electra Glide is the traditional Harley-David-son – complete with massive seat, sit-up handle-bars and footboards.

Designed for effortless cruising on America's long straight freeways, the vee-twin Harleys have built up a reputation throughout the world for rugged reliability – and in recent years handling and braking have been improved until they now compete with European and Japanese superbikes on level terms.

These then are the machines in the high-powered world of the superbike. Expensive, sophisticated, incredibly fast and with superb acceleration, they help motor cyclists all over the world to live out their dreams.

Latest in a line of 750cc four-cylinder models from
Honda is the CB750 Super Sport

Road racing machines

180 mph on two wheels! It takes some imagining but that is the speed top competitors are very close to achieving in the three forms of motor-cycle sport held on surfaced tracks: road racing, endurance racing and drag racing.

Oldest and widest spread of the three is road racing. This dates back to the turn of the century and for many years was run on genuine road circuits, which were closed for practising and racing but open the rest of the year to everyday traffic.

Prime example of a road racing course is the TT circuit in the Isle of Man. This twists and turns around the island for 37.7 miles and contains all the normal hazards you find while riding on the road: stone walls, houses, kerb-stones, hump-back bridges and all manner of corners from fast curves to slow hairpins.

This natural type of circuit was pre-eminent until the sixties. Then various factors combined to force racing off the road circuit and onto the purpose-built tracks on which the majority of 'road' races are now held. Most telling of these was safety – both for the crowd and the riders. Organisers found it increasingly difficult effectively to protect road-side spectators as speeds went up. At the same time the competitors began to demand that better safety precautions be taken to safeguard them in the event of a spill; safeguards such as run-off areas on corners and strawbales to pad trackside obstacles.

There are two main road racing series, the Formula 750 championship and the World Championship series. Both are organised by the Federation Internationale Motocycliste, governing body of motor-cycle sport throughout the world.

The Formula 750 series is relatively new, created to cater for the boom in large capacity machines. In an attempt to stop manufacturers building special works racers, the rules stipulate that at least twenty-five similar machines must have been made before any particular model can be raced.

Superchargers are not allowed and normal pump fuel must be used but apart from that there are few restrictions. Top bike in the class is the OW31 Yamaha.

The engine is a four-cylinder water-cooled, two-stroke unit that whacks out around 130 horse power and guzzles fuel at the rate of 12 miles per gallon. Weight has been cut to 320 lbs and top speed on the faster circuits, such as Daytona, is well over 170 mph.

Main rivals to the Yamahas, ridden so successfully by Americans Steve Baker and Kenny Roberts, Johnny Cecotto of Venezuela and Giacomo Agostini of Italy, are the Kawasakis and the Suzukis.

Both are powered by three-cylinder, water-cooled two-strokes. But neither factory have put a great effort into this class recently and with 'only' 120 horse power on tap, both are now outpaced by the brilliant Yamaha.

All Formula 750 races must be over at least 200 miles, and in the majority of cases the organisers prefer to run the events in two 100-mile legs, although Daytona, the original big-bike race, sticks to a single long race.

The engine that powered Barry Sheene to the 1976 500cc World Title, the RG500 Suzuki

The bike that took the 500 class by storm, the
RG500 Suzuki in the capable hands of Barry
Sheene in the Dutch TT

These relatively long races, allied to the heavy fuel consumption of the modern racing two-stroke, mean that refuelling stops are part of the Formula 750 scene. Using aircraft style fillers the practised pit crew can refill a five gallon tank in under five seconds!

This is very different from the World Championship series where, because of the number of different classes, shorter races are the order of the day.

Although major grands prix date back to the early twenties (and the Isle of Man TT was first run as long ago as 1907) it was not until 1949 that the championship series was started. Then five classes were held: 125cc, 250cc, 350cc and 500cc solos plus sidecars with a 500cc limit. In 1962 the 50cc class was added in recognition of the growing number of manufacturers who were building this category of machine for road use.

Superchargers, popular in the late thirties, were banned and the engines had to run on pump fuel which, in 1949 was only 75 octane! These rules still apply (though the octane rating has risen to 100) and during the intervening years others have been introduced to limit the amount of streamlining that may be fitted and, more recently, to limit the number of cylinders and gears.

Following a spate of accidents involving bikes using fairings enclosing the front wheel, it was decided, at the end of 1957, to limit streamlining to the present dolphin style with front-wheel exposed.

The restrictions on the number of cylinders and gears were introduced in the late sixties. Then the manufacturers seemed to be losing interest and it was feared that the development of multi-cylinder racers (a three-cylinder 50cc Suzuki was actually built and tested though never raced while Honda had a five-cylinder 125cc) might frighten off manufacturers with smaller budgets.

At the same time it was felt that something should be done about the number of gear ratios which, on some machines, had risen to as high as fourteen! These were needed because the engines had such a narrow power-band they had to have a multiplicity of gears if the rider was to keep the engine on the boil.

So the FIM decreed that in future the maximum number of speeds permitted would be six and that the 50cc class would be limited to single cylinder engines, the 125cc and 250cc to twins, while the 350cc and 500cc could have a maximum of four cylinders.

These rules were introduced at a time when Honda, Suzuki and Yamaha had all temporarily pulled out, so they hurt nobody and opened the way for today's highly competitive racing.

For, with way-out multi-cylinder works racers banned, racing in the seventies has been more competitive than ever before, with riders all over the world able to get equally matched machinery – and such is progress that the modern over-the-counter and basically very simple twin-cylinder 350cc Yamaha is faster than the works 500cc MV Agusta and Honda racers of ten years ago.

Most impressive racer in World Championship road racing today is the four-cylinder RG500 Suzuki which in 1976 thrashed the MV Agusta and Yamaha opposition to such effect that Giacomo Agostini gave up the Italian racer and bought a Suzuki, while Johnny Cecotto refused to continue to race the works

The Harley-Davidson 250cc racing machine, the fastest in its class

The fastest race machine of 1976, Steve Baker's 750cc OW31 Yamaha

Yamaha, claiming it was too slow!

As the name implies the engine capacity is 500cc and it made its debut as a factory racer in 1974. After two seasons of development Suzuki sprang a surprise when they announced that they were to build a batch for sale in 1976.

They have been a brilliant success. Selling for around £4,000 they proved faster than any bike ever offered for sale for the class and literally took over, filling the top places at virtually all the grands prix.

The two-stroke engine has the four-cylinders arranged in a square with induction controlled by disc-valves. A clever feature is that each cylinder constitutes a separate unit – and each can be dismantled and replaced without disturbing the other three.

Peak power is around 105 brake horse power

(10,500 rpm) which, driving through the six-speed gearbox, is enough to propel the RG500 and rider at about 170 mph.

Current top dog in both the 350cc and 250cc classes is little Walter Villa, the quiet and unassuming Italian who rides for Harley-Davidson. His water-cooled, twin-cylinder, two-stroke racers are made at the Italian subsidiary of the famous American company and they started life as straightforward copies of the super-successful Yamaha twins.

By patient development work allied to a super professional team of race mechanics, the Harleys improved steadily until in 1976 they snatched both titles from their Japanese rivals, who made the mistake of leaving it to the private owners instead of fielding a factory team.

Outwardly identical the engines have bore

and stroke dimensions of 64×54 mm and 56×50.5 mm, rev to 11,000 and 12,000 respectively, and produce 70 and 56 horse power.

So far Harley's attempts to produce a replica model for sale have been a disaster and the bulk of the fields in both the classes are made up of Yamaha racers, the incredibly successful twins from the Japanese factory.

It was Yamaha who, in the late sixties, pioneered the way with simple and relatively inexpensive twin-cylinder, two-strokes as competitive over-the-counter racers and the sport owes the Japanese company a great deal. For they filled the gap left by the demise of the British-built AJS, Matchless and Norton racers and have enabled riders all over the world to compete on purpose-built racers capable of holding their own against the best racers produced by rival factories.

The latest Yamahas have water-cooled engines and cantilever rear suspension but the engines remain very simple, twin-cylinder two-strokes. The 350cc (64×54 mm, 10,000 rpm and up to 70 bhp) is capable of close to 160 mph and the 250cc (54×54 mm, 10,500 rpm and up to 55 bhp) of around 150 mph.

In the 125cc class the Italian Morbidelli factory now outclass all rivals, their neat and very compact disc-valve, two-stroke twin capable of speeds up to 140 mph.

Designed by West German Jörg Möller for racing enthusiast Giancarlo Morbidelli (the factory make wood-working machinery) they won the World Championship in 1975 and again in 1976 and 100 replica models have been built and sold.

Morbidelli expanded into the 250cc and 350cc classes in 1976 with experimental engines, enlarged versions of their 125cc twin. In the smallest of the three classes they were challenged by the Spanish Bultaco factory who made a triumphant return to racing after a ten year absence when Angel Nieto took the 50cc crown on their smaller machine.

Taking a short cut Bultaco took over the Italian Piovaticci racing team complete with designer Jan Thiel of Holland and his frameman Martin Mijwaart. This enabled the Spanish company to step straight into racing (with improved versions of the 1975 Piovaticcis) and the 50cc single-cylinder, two-stroke (with water-cooling) proved good enough, in Nieto's capable hands, to win.

The best 50s now produce over 20 horse power and have a top speed of over 120 mph, fast enough to lap the Belgian Grand Prix circuit at an average of 100 mph despite a dead-stop hairpin and quite severe gradients.

From the tiddlers of racing to the giants – the new generation of big four-strokes now being produced by the factories for long-distance endurance racing, the new shop-window and battleground for the major manufacturers.

Forced out of World Championship road racing by the rising star of the two-strokes, Honda have long wanted to get back into big-time competition. But with the fashion swinging against two-strokes as road machines they saw no point in spending money on developing two-stroke racers when their bread and butter lay in four-strokes.

Finland's Tepi Lansivuori aboard his works 500cc Suzuki

So when endurance racing began to take off with crowds of over 100,000 at the French Bol d'Or 24-hour race, Honda decided to join in – and in 1976 they sent a forty-strong team to Europe to service an équipe of mighty 940cc four-cylinder racers.

Kawasaki, whose four-cylinder engines in Franco-Swiss frames had dominated the endurance scene for two seasons, were taken by surprise and Honda swept the long-distance board.

The 940cc Hondas have double-overhead-camshaft engines and are capable of 160 mph. But they are heavy and in short distance events are no match for the two-stroke racers.

This form of racing is now at the cross-roads. So far, apart from the Bol d'Or, the public have shown little interest in it and unless the factories sign the superstars, spectators are likely to shun it in favour of the more exciting short-distance road races with their slickly run programmes of different classes.

The third branch of two-wheeler sport run on a surfaced track is drag racing. This is an American variation on the old established British sprinting. Basically it is a contest between two riders to see who can cover a quarter-mile from a standing start in the shortest time. Contestants have gone to incredible lengths to cut their times to 8s, crossing the finish line at speeds up to 180 mph – and remember that the line is just 440 yards from the starting pad!

All the top men now use multi-engined bikes.

The new challenger from Honda, the four-cylinder 940cc which won the 1976 endurance championship

The latest contender for the 250cc championship, the Italian Morbidelli twin

American Russ Collins rides a triple (three 750cc four-cylinder engines) Honda, compatriot Tom Christenson has a double (2 × 830cc) Norton and top Britain John Hobbs a twin-engined (2 × 850cc) Weslake.

All use potent fuel mixes which include high percentages of nitro and methanol, and Hobbs, like all the top Europeans, has a supercharger as well. The power is transmitted via robust two-speed gearboxes and massively wide slick (treadless) rear tyres which they warm up before a run to make them tacky for a scorching getaway.

It is a hectic, noisy and colourful sport which has established its own following both in the States and in England, though it is virtually unknown in Europe apart from occasional meetings in Holland and Sweden.

Sidecar action in the 1976 Austrian GP

America's most powerful dragster, Russ Collins' triple-engined 3600cc Honda

John Hobbs in July 1975, on his first 8-second run

The American Tom C Christenson riding Hogslayer, 'the most successful drag bike ever', in January 1976

Off-road competition machines

The versatility of the motor cycle is well illustrated by the many sporting uses to which it is put. For, apart from road racing and drag racing, three other major sports are contested on motor cycles.

Most popular and widespread of these is motocross, or to give it its original British name, scrambling. This is racing on a circuit (usually about a mile long) laid out on rough ground.

The courses normally include a number of jumps and a lot of tight corners. A water splash may be included too but in recent years the circuits have tended to get faster and easier.

The surface starts as grass but after a few races this is torn up and mud, sand and dust are the order of the day. To reduce the risk of injury from stones flung up by an opponent's rear wheel, competitors wear plastic face masks and shoulder and chest guards similar to those used by ice hockey players.

They also wear padded leather trousers and massive boots. Their motor cycles are single-cylinder 500cc, 250cc or 125cc machines; all two-strokes except for the British CCM which continues to do battle in the biggest class.

The accent is on lightness coupled to the best possible suspension to soak up the body-jarring bumps. For motocross is the most physically demanding of two-wheeled motor-sport and requires a high standard of fitness from its top competitors.

The sport started at about the same time, the twenties, in both England and Belgium. It boomed after the war, especially on the Continent where it was put on a professional basis with permanent circuits and paid organisers.

In the sixties it spread to North America where it has made tremendous strides in the last five years. There is a World Championship for each of the three classes and a European title for the winner of the sidecar division, the newest branch of the sport.

The three-wheelers are limited to 1000cc and with little or no factory interest the contestants have shown a great deal of ingenuity in building competitive machinery. The most popular engine is still the 830cc Norton, used by three-times champion Robert Grogg of Switzerland and by two of his closest challengers, Nick Thompson of England and Austria's Bruno Schneider.

Running motocross very close in the popularity stakes is speedway, the most professional of all motor-cycle sport. The basic idea of speedway is simplicity itself – 500cc motor cycles racing round a loose surfaced track which measures anything from 120 (these very short tracks are popular in America) to 600 metres.

The normal length of European circuits is 350 metres and the surface is shale, watered before racing to bind it and to keep the dust down. The sport was started in Australia and was brought to Europe by Johnny Hoskins the grand old man of speedway who is still promoting at Canterbury though now well over eighty! He brought the sport to Europe in 1928 and the first meeting was on a track behind a pub at High Beech in Epping Forest. The interest was enormous and soon league racing was an established part of the British sporting scene.

Like other sports it boomed after the war when crowds of over 80,000 used to pack

Motocross, American-style at Daytona in 1976

Wembley Stadium for league matches. It slumped in the fifties and all but died in England with the number of tracks sinking to single figures.

Many wrote off speedway, but it refused to die. In the sixties it began to pick up, and helped by steady growth in Europe it has gone on expanding; in 1977 the number of league clubs in the British Isles totals around forty.

It is also strong in Sweden, Poland and Russia, with other successful tracks operating in America (where a league was established in California in 1976), New Zealand, Australia, South Africa as well as in most European countries.

The machines are built for lightness and for control when the riders power-slide them round the corners, using the engine to spin the rear wheel, causing it to slide out and round in an arc.

Running on alcohol fuels the single cylinder four-stroke engines produce around 55 horse power. There are no gear boxes – and no brakes. The riders slow for the corners by shutting the throttle and putting the bike into a two-wheel drift.

They then open the throttle and broadside around the corner, a fantastic sight, especially when you have four top men separated by just a few inches – or less. Races are normally over four laps from a standing, clutch start from behind an electrically operated gate which springs up when the referee, who controls the meeting, flicks a switch.

League racing, between teams of seven riders (six men plus a reserve) is the backbone of the sport but individual events, of which the World Championship is the most important, are the showpieces.

For over thirty years British-built JAP (J. A. Prestwich of Tottenham) engines ruled the roost. Then the Czech-built Eso, later absorbed by Jawa, took over, but in 1976 Britain hit back when British riders on British-built Weslakes dominated the international scene, Peter Collins winning the World Championship with Malcolm Simmons in second place.

Three sports similar to speedway are sand-track, grass-track and ice-speedway. Sand-track, popular in West Germany, Norway, Czechoslovakia and Yugoslavia, is held on longer tracks, usually about 1,000 metres.

The machines are basically speedway bikes but rear suspension is added to improve handling at the higher speeds (up to 120 mph) reached on the longer straights and brakes are obligatory because, although not normally used, they are a safety factor if things go wrong.

Grass-track is virtually speedway racing on a grass circuit. Like the long-track bikes, grass-track machines are fitted with rear suspension and two-speed gearboxes, first gear for starting and second for the rest of the race.

Ice racing lays a strong claim to being the most spectacular form of motor-cycle competition. Again the bikes are basically speedway machines, powered by 500cc single-cylinder alcohol-burning Jawa, JAP or Weslake engines, but the tyres are studded with 25 mm spikes.

These grip the ice so well that the bikes do not slide even when power is applied. Instead the rider lays the bike right over on the corners until

Motocross sidecar action from the 1975 European champion, Dutchman Ton Van Heugten (Yamaha-Hagon)

The 250 Motocross Honda   Ice speedway machines on one of the Dutch tracks

his left knee, with leg trailing, skims the ice surface.

The oval tracks are usually about 300 metres long and because of the danger of the spikes a race is normally confined to three competitors who cover three laps. The sport has boomed in Russia and is also held in Sweden, West Germany, Czechoslovakia, France and in Holland where a special track, with under-circuit freezing equipment, has been built at Assen, headquarters town of the Dutch TT.

Completely different from ice-speedway and from every other form of motor-cycle sport is trials, the only competitive branch of the sport in which speed plays no part. In fact very often

the ability to go as slowly as possible pays off. For the whole point of trials riding is to negotiate a marked course without touching the ground with a foot, or worse still with both feet.

A normal trial consists of a number of sections, often marked with white tape, connected by a marked route on normal roads or tracks. Competitors start at intervals and follow the directions to the first section.

This could be a steep climb over seemingly impassable rocks, a ride along a stream bed or a tricky descent down a muddy slope. Whatever the hazard it has to be attempted before the competitor continues to the next section.

An official observer is at every section and

marks each rider according to how he fares: no marks lost if he 'cleans' the section, one if he 'dabs' (touches the ground with one foot once), three if he 'foots' (touches more than once) or five if he stops or rides out of the section before reaching the 'section ends' cards.

Trials are immensely popular in the United Kingdom where up to twenty trials, each involving up to a hundred riders, are held every weekend. Recently the sport has become popular on the Continent and in America and the creation of a World Championship has accelerated this interest.

In the fifties 500cc single-cylinder four-strokes dominated the scene. The bikes were built to be as light as possible, with massive ground clearance to clear rocks and tree trunks.

In the sixties came a swing to the lighter two-strokes, spearheaded by the Spanish Bultaco factory who signed Irish ace Sammy Miller (who made his name on a 500cc Ariel) to ride and develop their machine.

The move proved so successful that the new range of single-cylinder two-strokes (first with 250cc engines and later with 350cc engines) took over with other Spanish factories such as Montesa and Ossa joining in.

Now the Spanish two-strokes dominate the scene, although Miller recently joined Honda and is now helping the Japanese factory to develop a four-stroke to beat the Spaniards.

Latest from Bultaco is the 125cc 'Mini Sherpa'

Denmark's speedway superstar Ole Olsen shows how it's done at Wembley

Slow speed concentration as Graham Cross tackles a trials section on his Bultaco

Choppers and stunt bikes

Dave Taylor in his famous wheelie act

The motor-cycle scene is fringed with exotic machines and way-out characters, and few will argue that Evel Kneivel is the 'daddy' of them all when it comes to getting an image across.

For Evel (real name Robert) is a name known to more people throughout the world than any other motor cyclist. If you are one of the few who have not heard of him, Evel is the world's greatest stuntman on two wheels.

He made his name leaping motor cycles (he currently has a contract with Harley-Davidson but in the past he has used Laverda and Triumph machines) over cars and buses. During the course of his hectic career he has broken just about every bone in his body, but he has made a pile of cash.

Unfortunately his most famous stunt, attempting to jump the Snake River Canyon in a rocket, ended in abject failure and detracted from the many genuinely incredible stunts he had performed on real motor cycles.

However, Evel remains stuntman supreme and for a long time now we are likely to read of others 'beating' his records. One record they are not likely to beat is the amount of the money he made doing it.

A very different character, with a very different act, is England's Dave Taylor. This quietly spoken Londoner has developed a series of motor-cycle stunts, and he now travels all over Europe to give shows, often during the intervals at major car and motor-cycle race meetings.

His original act was centred on his ability to wheelie (ride with the front wheel high in the air) amazing distances and at high speed, negotiating corners and gradients. Now he has developed other acts, including standing on the

Uneven weight distribution from a typical US
chopper rider

Evel Knievel at Wembley in May 1975

tank and controlling the bike while leaning way out over the front wheel!

American Don Vesco has a very different approach. He lies flat on his back and is currently the holder of the outright speed record for motor cycles – at just over 300 mph.

Like Dave Taylor, Don is quiet spoken, wears spectacles, and plans things down to the last detail. He built his streamlined record breaker himself, and prepares the Yamaha engines in his workshop in El Cajon near San Diego in Southern California.

His original streamliner was powered by two 350cc Yamaha racing engines, and with these Don took the record at over 280 mph. Then, when Yamaha started to sell the four-cylinder TZ750 racers, Don bought two of those and shoe-horned them into the frame.

Like all recent record-breaking two-wheelers the Vesco machine looks like an enlarged cigar. The rider lies on his back behind the front wheel with his head in a tiny, aircraft-style blister atop the fuselage.

The two engines are mounted, one behind the other, astern of the rider with the rear wheel behind them. The idea is to present the smallest possible frontal area, and the diameter of the body is less than two feet. Equipment includes a built-in fire fighting system and twin braking parachutes, one of which is triggered automatically if the machine leans beyond a certain angle.

All recent record breaking has been done at the Bonneville Salt Flats near Salt Lake City in America. There, in the autumn when the salt flats are dry, they grade the surface smooth and mark a straight up to eleven miles long.

Another American phenomenon is the chopper, the rakish looking motor cycle made famous

A monster cruiser from the US highways, a Harley-Davidson 'full dresser'

by the film *Easy Rider*. The most noticeable feature of a chopper is the elongated front fork and small front wheel. Then there are the high swept-back handlebars, the tilted seat and the forward mounted footrests which give the characteristic armchair riding position.

In the States the chopper is a cult and riders spend a lot of dollars, time and ingenuity to make their machine as perfect as they can. Originally, nearly all choppers were powered by big-twin Harley-Davidson engines but now any big engine will do.

Every nut and bolt is chromed and polished; tanks and frames are painted and lined with special colours, engines are stripped and rebuilt with crankcases buffed until they glisten, and cylinder fins smoothed and painted. The work that goes into the better examples is awe inspiring. Having exhausted the potential of the chopper, some Americans have gone one further and built special three-wheelers powered either by a motor-cycle or a car engine.

A typical example spotted on the beach at Daytona, scene of the famous 200-mile race and home of the major chopper show which is held the day before the big race, was powered by a Pontiac vee-eight engine coupled to an automatic gearbox. The single tiny front wheel stuck out on a chopper-style front fork, and the rider sat behind the engine in a beautifully decorated cab between two huge rear wheels shod with racing car slick tyres.

It had taken the owner four years to build and had cost him £3,000 plus the time. Asked why he had done it he replied, with a smile: 'Well you could say it's just a hobby. I guess I enjoy it.' A sentence which explains the magic of motor cycling in all its varied forms.

Index